ASTERIX THE GAUL

TEXT BY GOSCINNY

DRAWINGS BY UDERZO

TRANSLATED BY ANTHEA BELL AND DEREK HOCKRIDGE

HODDER AND STOUGHTON

LONDON   SYDNEY   AUCKLAND

692288

Asterix the Gaul

ISBN 0 340 04240 0 (cased)
ISBN 0 340 17210 x (limp)

Copyright © Dargaud Editeur 1961, Goscinny-Uderzo
English language text copyright © Brockhampton Press Ltd 1969
(now Hodder Children's Books)

First pubished in Great Britain 1969 (cased)
This impression 110 109 108 107
First published in Great Britain 1973 (limp)
This impression 114 113 112

Published by Hodder Dargaud Ltd,
338 Euston Road, London NW1 3BH

Printed in Belgium by Proost International Book production

GAULISH VILLAGE

COMPENDIUM

LAUDANUM

AQUARIUM

TOTORUM

BELGICA

LUTETIA

SPQR

ARMORICA

GAUL
(ROMAN CONQUEST)
50 B.C.

CELTICA

PROVINCIA

AQUITANIA

The year is 50 BC. Gaul is entirely occupied by the Romans. Well, not entirely... One small village of indomitable Gauls still holds out against the invaders. And life is not easy for the Roman legionaries who garrison the fortified camps of Totorum, Aquarium, Laudanum and Compendium...

a few of the Gauls

Asterix, the hero of these adventures. A shrewd, cunning little warrior; all perilous missions are immediately entrusted to him. Asterix gets his superhuman strength from the magic potion brewed by the druid Getafix…

Obelix, Asterix's inseparable friend. A menhir delivery-man by trade; addicted to wild boar. Obelix is always ready to drop everything and go off on a new adventure with Asterix — so long as there's wild boar to eat, and plenty of fighting.

Getafix, the venerable village druid. Gathers mistletoe and brews magic potions. His speciality is the potion which gives the drinker superhuman strength. But Getafix also has other recipes up his sleeve…

Cacofonix, the bard. Opinion is divided as to his musical gifts. Cacofonix thinks he's a genius. Everyone else thinks he's unspeakable. But so long as he doesn't speak, let alone sing, everybody likes him…

Finally, Vitalstatistix, the chief of the tribe. Majestic, brave and hot-tempered, the old warrior is respected by his men and feared by his enemies. Vitalstatistix himself has only one fear; he is afraid the sky may fall on his head tomorrow. But as he always says, 'Tomorrow never comes.'

IN THE YEAR 50 BC, AFTER A LONG STRUGGLE, THE ANCIENT GAULS HAD BEEN CONQUERED BY THE ROMANS.....

CHIEFS LIKE VERCINGETORIX HAD TO LAY THEIR ARMS AT CAESAR'S FEET....

OUCH!

CLANG!

PEACE REIGNS, DISTURBED ONLY BY OCCASIONAL ATTACKS BY THE GERMANS, SPEEDILY REPULSED....

So! But ve komm back!

Gut! Ve go!

ALL GAUL IS OCCUPIED....

BELGICA

ARMORICA

S.P.Q.R.

CELTICA

AQUITANIA

PROVINCIA

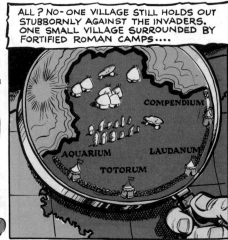

ALL? NO-ONE VILLAGE STILL HOLDS OUT STUBBORNLY AGAINST THE INVADERS. ONE SMALL VILLAGE SURROUNDED BY FORTIFIED ROMAN CAMPS....

COMPENDIUM

AQUARIUM

LAUDANUM

TOTORUM

ALL EFFORTS TO SUBDUE THESE PROUD GAULS HAVE FAILED, AND CAESAR ASKS HIMSELF....

QUID?

AND NOW WE MEET OUR HERO, THE WARRIOR ASTERIX, JUST OFF HUNTING AS USUAL

BACK SOON, ASTERIX?

I'LL BE BACK FOR DINNER, OBELIX

HERE HE COMES!

WE'LL GET HIM

IPSO FACTO!

SIC!

BIFF!

OW!

BANG!

OUCH!

ACCIDENCE WILL HAPPEN....

VAE VICTO VAE VICTIS!

WE DECLINE!

5

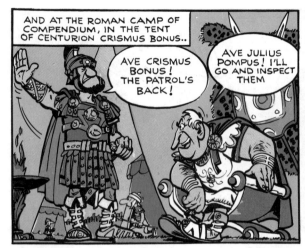

AND AT THE ROMAN CAMP OF COMPENDIUM, IN THE TENT OF CENTURION CRISMUS BONUS..

AVE CRISMUS BONUS! THE PATROL'S BACK!

AVE JULIUS POMPUS! I'LL GO AND INSPECT THEM

AVE....

?!?.?

WHAT HAPPENED, BY ALL THE GODS? WERE YOU ATTACKED BY SUPERIOR NUMBERS?

SUPERIOR NUMBERS...

CAN'T QUITE SAY...

THERE WAS ONE OF THEM...

NOT A VERY LARGE ONE EITHER!

BY JUPITER! THERE MUST BE SOME SECRET BEHIND THE SUPERHUMAN STRENGTH OF THESE GAULS!

MEANWHILE....

SO YOU'RE BACK ASTERIX. ANYTHING INTERESTING HAPPEN?

NO....

OH YES! I KNOCKED FOUR ROMANS OUT

OH, GOOD!

WANT TO HELP ME EAT MY BOAR?

JUST COMING! I'VE GOT TWO MORE MENHIRS TO DELIVER

HERE IS THE POTION THAT MAKES THE DRINKER INVINCIBLE! IT INCREASES HIS STRENGTH TENFOLD—FOR A LIMITED PERIOD OF TIME

WHAT'S THE RECIPE, O DRUID?

THE ORIGIN OF THIS RECIPE IS LOST IN THE MISTS OF TIME. IT IS HANDED DOWN FROM DRUID TO DRUID BY WORD OF MOUTH....

ALL I CAN REVEAL IS THAT THERE'S MISTLETOE AND LOBSTER IN IT....

THE LOBSTER IS OPTIONAL, BUT IT IMPROVES THE FLAVOUR!

SPLOSH!

CAN I HAVE SOME?

NO, OBELIX, YOU CAN NOT AND WELL YOU KNOW IT!

YOU FELL INTO THE CAULDRON WHEN YOU WERE A BABY, AND IT HAD A PERMANENT EFFECT ON YOU, IT WOULD BE DANGEROUS FOR YOU TO DRINK ANY MORE!

THANKS, O DRUID!

IT'S NOT FAIR, BY BELENOS!

OW! OW! OW!

I'VE TOLD YOU BEFORE NOT TO SHAKE HANDS WITH ME WHEN YOU'VE JUST HAD YOUR POTION

HE'S RIGHT, I DON'T KNOW MY OWN STRENGTH!

WE'VE BEEN LAYING SIEGE TO THESE GAULS FOR YEARS! THEY'VE GOT A NERVE! THIS MORNING'S PROVOCATION IS GOING TOO FAR. ONE AGAINST FOUR IS NO JOKE! THEY'RE MAKING US LOOK RIDICULOUS

THERE'S SOME MYSTERY BEHIND THE STRENGTH OF THESE GAULS. WE MUST LEARN THEIR SECRET

YOU'RE RIGHT, MARCUS GINANTONICUS! WE MUST LEARN THEIR SECRET, AND FAST! CAESAR HAS INDICATED HIS DISPLEASURE ALL THE WAY FROM ROME. WE NEED A SPY IN THE GAULS' VILLAGE. I WANT A VOLUNTEER!

?!

AS THERE ARE SO MANY VOLUNTEERS, WE'LL HAVE TO PLAY MUSICAL CHAIRS TO PICK THE SPY!

THIS ANCIENT ROMAN GAME IS PLAYED WITH ONE LESS CHAIR THAN THERE ARE LEGIONARIES.....

...WHEN THE MUSIC STOPS.....

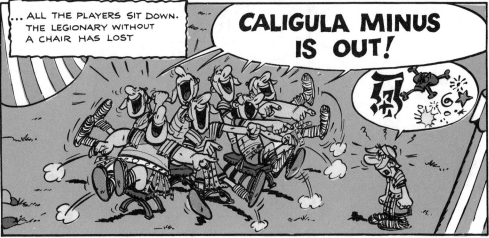

... ALL THE PLAYERS SIT DOWN. THE LEGIONARY WITHOUT A CHAIR HAS LOST

CALIGULA MINUS IS OUT!

I'M NOT GOING TO SPY ON THE GAULS!

CAESAR WILL BE ETERNALLY GRATEFUL TO YOU IF YOU GO, CALIGULA MINUS!

I AM NOT GOING TO SPY ON THE GAULS!

I'LL ROAST YOU ALIVE IF YOU DON'T!

OH, ALL RIGHT, I'LL GO AND SPY ON THE GAULS!

GET HIM UP LIKE A GAUL!

MEANWHILE, IN THE GAULISH VILLAGE...

THOSE ROMANS HAVE KEPT QUIET TOO LONG! IT CAN'T LAST. BE ON YOUR GUARD— AND NEVER FORGET TO TAKE YOUR MAGIC POTION!

LONG LIVE OUR CHIEF VITALSTATISTIX!

CHIEF!

WHAT IS IT, OBELIX?

THEY WON'T LET ME HAVE ANY POTION. IT'S NOT FAIR! I FEEL RATHER WEAK...

HELP! HERE COMES THE BARD CACOFONIX!

I WILL NOW GIVE YOU A SONG TO INSPIRE THE WARRIORS WITH COURAGE...

CAN'T STOP...

I'VE GOT NO END OF MENHIRS TO DELIVER...

MAY THE SKY FALL ON MY HEAD! IT'S GETTING LATE

BARBARIANS! THEY DON'T APPRECIATE MY ART!

WAIT A MINUTE!

HM?

SSH!

BUT...

I CAN HEAR FOOTSTEPS— CHAINS CLANKING— SOMEONE WAILING!

!

LET'S HIDE AT THE TOP OF THIS TREE! WE MAY SOON BE LOOSENING UP OUR MUSCLES!

BY ALL THE GODS, I SHOULD HAVE STAYED AT HOME! I NEVER OUGHT TO HAVE JOINED CAESAR'S LEGIONS IN SEARCH OF FAME AND FORTUNE! MY SKIN'S NOT WORTH A SESTERTIUS AND I'LL NEVER EAT TAPIOCA (I) LIKE MOTHER MADE AGAIN!

(I) SPAGHETTI WAS NOT IMPORTED FROM CHINA BY MARCO POLO UNTIL MUCH LATER.

WILL YOU SHUT UP, CALIGULA MINUS! AFTER ALL, WHEN THE HORDES OF GAULS ATTACK US YOU'RE THE ONLY ONE THEY'LL SPARE!

SURE ENOUGH, THERE ARE THE HORDES..

ROMANS, WITH A GAUL AS PRISONER!

WE'LL RESCUE HIM!

12

RIGHT! EVERYONE GOT IT? IF THEY ATTACK WE ONLY PUT UP A TOKEN RESISTANCE!

HERE WE COME, BY TOUTATIS!

HERE THEY COME, BY JUPITER!

THEY'RE A BIT SOFT TODAY, DON'T YOU THINK?

YES, THEY'RE OFF FORM. THEY SHOULD TAKE CARE OF THEMSELVES — EAT A WELL BALANCED DIET

PAF!

CLONG!

THAT'S THE LOT...

COULDN'T WE BRING THEM ROUND AND START AGAIN?

NO, COME ON! IT'S GETTING LATE

MI — MISSION ACCOMPLISHED!

WE WILL STRIKE OFF YOUR CHAINS!

BUT YOU'LL NEED TOOLS.... A HAMMER!

HA! HA! WE'RE THE TOOLS!

!

WHAT'S YOUR NAME?

CALIG...ER...CALIGULIMINIX I'M FROM LUTETIA. I WAS JUST GOING ON HOLIDAY TO ARMORICA WHEN THE ROMANS CAPTURED ME

BUT EVERYWHERE ELSE THE ROMANS AND THE GAULS ARE AT PEACE!

YES, BUT I LOOK SO CLEVER AND CUNNING THAT IN THEIR EYES I WAS A SPY

THEIR EYES CAN'T BE ALL THAT BRIGHT! HA! HA!

MARCUS GINANTONICUS AND HIS HEROIC DETACHMENT RETURN TO COMPENDIUM....

TCHIC! BLDZRRZLM MIDLXVIIM NIZDRC

THE GAULS CAME AND SAW AND CONQUERED CALIGULA MINUS!

A GREAT VICTORY FOR US!

LET'S HOPE CALIGULA MINUS GETS BACK IN ONE PIECE TO TELL US WHAT HE'S SEEN!

HE'D BETTER! IF NOT I'LL HAVE SOMETHING TO SAY TO HIS ROMAN REMAINS!

ALEA JACTA EST!

PARDON?

MEANWHILE....

THIS IS OUR VILLAGE, CALIGULIMINIX. YOU'LL BE SAFE HERE! IT'S FULL OF GAULS!

THAT'S A GREAT COMFORT

ASTERIX AND OBELIX ARE BACK!

THEY'VE GOT SOMETHING WITH THEM!

SOMETHING VERY PECULIAR, BY BELENOS!

COME AND MEET OUR CHIEF, VITALSTATISTIX

BUT— BUT THEY'RE ALL ARMED!

YES, WE HAVE TO BE PREPARED TO FIGHT THE ROMANS AT THE DROP OF A HELMET

A WISE PRECAUTION!

OUR CHIEF VITALSTATISTIX IS IN THERE WITH GETAFIX THE DRUID. THEY'VE HEARD YOU'RE HERE

WELCOME, BROTHER! MAKE YOURSELF AT HOME!

AV...ER... HOW DO YOU DO?

I WILL NOW SING A SONG OF WELCOME!

JUST GO AND LOOK UP AN OAK TREE TO SEE IF I'M THERE!

TAKE A STROLL ROUND THE VILLAGE TILL DINNER TIME. BUT DON'T GO TOO FAR. THERE ARE ROMANS ABOUT

RIGHT!

I WONDER WHAT SORT OF TOOLS THEY USE FOR WORKING METAL...

FULLIAUTOMATIX

WEAPONS FOR ALL THE FAMILY

BING! BONNG! CLING!

?

LLANG!

HIS HANDS, BY JUPITER! HIS BARE HANDS!

CLONG! CLING!

HOW'S THAT MENHIR GOING?

OH, IT'S COMING ALONG!

???

?

THEY CERTAINLY ARE VERY STRONG...MAYBE CRISMUS BONUS WAS RIGHT. THEY MUST HAVE SOME SECRET!

DINNER'S READY, CALIGULIMINIX. IT'S WILD BOAR!

IS THERE SOME SECRET BEHIND YOUR SUPERHUMAN STRENGTH?

EAT UP YOUR BOAR, IT'S GETTING COLD

YUM! YUM! YES BUT WE CAN'T REVEAL IT! SCRUNCH!

WHY CAN'T YOU REVEAL YOUR SECRET?

BECAUSE IT'S A SECRET!

THAT'S NOT FAIR! WHAT ARE THINGS COMING TO IF ONE GAUL CAN'T TRUST ANOTHER?

IF I WAS AS STRONG AS YOU I COULD GET THROUGH THE ROMAN LINES AND GO HOME TO LUTETIA!

MY POOR FAMILY! SNIFF! THEY'LL BE WORRIED TO DEATH!

WHAT DO WE DO NOW?

WE COULD ALWAYS EAT HIS WILD BOAR?

COME ON, CALIGULIMINIX! WE'RE GOING TO SEE THE DRUID

HE'LL BE UP AN OAK TREE. IT'S THE SIXTH DAY OF THE NEW MOON, AND MISTLETOE CUT THEN IS A POWERFUL ANTIDOTE TO POISON

HI, DRUID!

OUCH!

ASTERIX, I TOLD YOU BEFORE NOT TO MAKE ME JUMP WHEN I'M USING MY SICKLE!!!

WELL, WHAT DO YOU WANT?

I DON'T WANT ANYTHING. IT'S MY FRIEND CALIGULIMINIX— HE'D LIKE TO KNOW THE SECRET OF OUR SUPERHUMAN STRENGTH....

NOTHING DOING!

!

I HAVE TO GET HOME TO MY FAMILY.... GO BACK TO WORK....

WHAT DO YOU DO, ANYWAY?

ER... OH I'M A GUIDE. I SHOW BARBARIAN TOURISTS ROUND THE NIGHT LIFE OF LUTETIA...

WELL, WHAT ABOUT IT, DRUID?

NO, NO, AND FOR THE THIRD TIME, NO!

OH, FINE! THAT'S JUST FINE! I QUITE SEE!

I'LL TRY GOING HOME ALL THE SAME. AND IF THE ROMANS TAKE ME TO ROME FOR THE LIONS TO EAT ME IN THE CIRCUS, I'LL SAY IN BETWEEN EACH MOUTHFUL THE LIONS TAKE, 'IT'S ALL GETAFIX THE DRUID'S FAULT! IT'S ALL GETAFIX THE DRUID'S FAULT!'

OH, ALL RIGHT, ALL RIGHT!

COME BACK, CALIGULIMINIX!

I'LL SHOW YOU MY SECRET. I'LL EVEN LET YOU TASTE IT

IT'S A SECRET YOU CAN EAT?

COME ON, ALL OF YOU! OUR DRUID GETAFIX IS GOING TO MAKE THE MAGIC POTION!

ONE PORTION OF THIS POTION WILL GIVE YOU ALL THE STRENGTH YOU NEED TO GET HOME TO LUTETIA...

...BUT THE EFFECTS WILL WEAR OFF QUITE QUICKLY

NEVER MIND, I'LL SEE ABOUT STEALING THAT CAULDRON!

HERE'S THE POTION!

THIS POTION... I.... ER, I POTATE IT?

GLUG! GLUG! GLUG! GLUG! GLUG!

TASTES LIKE VEGETABLE SOUP!

IT COMES IN SEVERAL OTHER DELICIOUS FLAVOURS: SHRIMP, CHEESE OMELETTE, DUCK WITH ORANGE SAUCE AND VANILLA!

BUT I DON'T FEEL ANY DIFFERENT....

TRY LIFTING THAT ROCK OVER THERE!

THIS ONE? BUT I COULD NEVER...

?!!?

HA! HA! HA!

HA! HA!

HA! HA! HA! HA! HA! HA! HA!

THIS IS GREAT!

KERPLONK!

THE POTION MAKES YOU VERY STRONG, BUT NOT INVULNERABLE... I DO HAVE A RECIPE FOR THAT, BUT THAT'S ANOTHER STORY....

AND NOW I DECLARE THE REVELS OPEN!

HI, CACOFONIX, WE'RE WAITING FOR YOU!

COME ON, TENANSIX!

WHAT ARE WE GOING TO DO NOW?

DANCE!

TAKE YOUR PARTNERS! SET TO THE RIGHT— SET TO THE LEFT....

ONE LINE FORWARD, THE OTHER LINE BACK!

SET TO YOUR PARTNER, SHAKE HIM BY THE HAND!

PULL HIS MOUSTACHE!

PULL HIS MOUSTACHE! ?!?

WHAT ON EARTH IS THIS?

ER....IT'S A DETACHABLE MOUSTACHE! THE LATEST THING FROM LUTETIA!

I DON'T THINK YOU'RE A GAUL AT ALL! I BELIEVE YOU'RE A ROMAN SPY!

GET HIM!

?!

IT'S NO USE GOING AFTER HIM. HE'S JUST HAD THE POTION; HE'S PRACTICALLY INVINCIBLE!

SO HE'S ESCAPING, THANKS TO YOUR POTION!

BY MY GOLDEN SICKLE, IT WAS YOU WHO WANTED ME TO GIVE HIM SOME!

WELL, NEVER MIND! THAT SPY DIDN'T LEARN MUCH, AND THE EFFECTS OF THE POTION WILL SOON WEAR OFF!

MEANWHILE CALIGULA MINUS MAKES FULL SPEED FOR THE ROMAN CAMP OF COMPENDIUM

HALT! QUO VADIS, GAUL?

BOING!

20

22

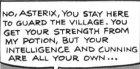

SOON AFTERWARDS IN THE GAULISH VILLAGE

I'M JUST GOING TO PICK SOME MISTLETOE IN THE FOREST

WANT ME TO COME WITH YOU, DRUID?

NO, ASTERIX, YOU STAY HERE TO GUARD THE VILLAGE. YOU GET YOUR STRENGTH FROM MY POTION, BUT YOUR INTELLIGENCE AND CUNNING ARE ALL YOUR OWN...

IT WOULD BE A DISASTER FOR US TO LOSE YOU! BESIDES, I'LL BE BACK SOON

GOOD...

♫ (1)

1 ANCIENT GAULISH AIR

OOPS!

GOT HIM!

⚡💥👊💀 (2)

(2) ANCIENT GAULISH SWEAR-WORDS

SOON AFTERWARDS

WE GOT THE DRUID, O CRISMUS BONUS!

GOOD WORK, TULLIUS OCTOPUS!

AS A REWARD YOU SHALL HAVE 100 SESTERTII, AND YOU CAN GO TO ROME ON LEAVE TO SEE THE CIRCUS!

GOODY GOODY GUMDROPS! I'M GOING TO THE CIRCUS!

NOW, DRUID, YOU WILL TELL ME YOUR SECRET!

THAT'S WHAT YOU THINK!

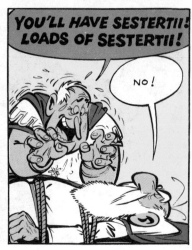

25

HERE WE ARE IN THE CAMP! ARE YOU GOING TO PLAY YOUR PRACTICAL JOKE NOW?

NO, IT'S GETTING DARK. I'LL WAIT TILL MORNING, IT'LL BE FUNNIER THEN

OH!

GOOD NIGHT!

SOON AFTERWARDS

AND NOW TO FIND WHERE THEY'VE GOT THE DRUID...

ZZZZZ

LET'S HAVE A LOOK OVER HERE...

RECLINE AND HAVE A BITE TO EAT, O MARCUS GINANTONICUS, MY TRUSTY NUMBER TWO. I WANT A WORD WITH YOU!

THANKS, O CRISMUS BONUS!

WE MUST GET THE DRUID'S RECIPE! WITH IT WE SHALL BE INVINCIBLE. WE CAN GO TO ROME AND TAKE OVER FROM CAESAR!

JULIUS CAESAR?

PRECISELY, **JULIUS**! THE TWO OF US WILL FORM A TRIUMVIRATE!

I NEED YOU NOW, BUT AFTERWARDS I'LL BE THE TRIUMVIRATE ON MY OWN!

I'LL HAVE HIM THROWN TO THE LIONS, AND THEN I ALONE WILL BE CAESAR!

clic!

27

28

O CRISMUS BONUS!

NOW WHAT?

WE'VE CAPTURED A GAUL IN THE DRUID'S TENT BUT WE NEED REINFORCEMENTS TO STOP THE PRISONER GETTING AWAY!!!

BY JUPITER! SOUND THE ALARM!

TANTANTARA TATA!

SOON AFTERWARDS

SURRENDER, GAUL! OR I GIVE THE ORDER TO ATTACK!

WELL IS HE SURRENDERING OR ISN'T HE?

ALL THIS WAITING IS GETTING ME DOWN!

WATCH OUT! HERE HE COMES!

I LAY DOWN MY WEAPON AT YOUR FEET, CENTURION, AS OUR CHIEF VERCINGETORIX LAID HIS ARMS AT THE FEET OF YOUR MASTER CAESAR!

ZING!

CLANG!

CLINK!

CLONK!

CLICK

CLACK!

WHOOSH!

WELL, COME ON, DO SOMETHING! I SURRENDER! I CAN'T HANG ABOUT ALL DAY!

IT'S DAYS SINCE THE MESSENGERS LEFT TO LOOK FOR STRAWBERRIES, AND NOT ONE HAS TURNED UP YET!

THE MESSENGERS ARE BACK, O CRISMUS BONUS!

ABOUT TIME!

AVE CRISMUS BONUS!

AVE, AVE, BOYS! THE STRAWBERRIES — DID YOU GET THEM?

NO.

NOT A STRAWBERRY

WE LOOKED EVERYWHERE!

TULLIUS OCTOPUS ISN'T BACK YET

HERE I AM, O CRISMUS BONUS!

I FOUND STRAWBERRIES, O CRISMUS BONUS! I BOUGHT THEM FOR A VAST SUM FROM A GREEK MERCHANT I HAPPENED TO MEET!

GIVE THEM HERE!

THIS TIME I REALLY MEAN IT! AS A REWARD YOU CAN GO HOME ON LEAVE TO SEE ALL THE FUN OF THE CIRCUS!

I'M GOING TO THE CIRCUS! I'M GOING TO THE CIRCUS!

DRUID! HERE ARE THE STRAWBERRIES YOU ORDERED FOR THE MAGIC POTION!

WHAT DO YOU THINK OF THEM, ASTERIX?

NOT UP TO MUCH!

!

NOT BAD...

HM...

COME TO THINK OF IT, THOSE WERE EXCELLENT STRAWBERRIES!

YES, JUST THE SORT I NEED. GO AND GET ME SOME MORE

35

OUR ROAD TO ROME IS CLEAR, O MARCUS GINANTONICUS! CAESAR'S DAYS ARE NUMBERED!

DRUID, GIVE US THAT RECIPE IN WRITING!

AND THEN WE'LL GET RID OF THESE TWO GAULS! IT WILL TEACH THEM A LESSON!

HERE'S HAIR ON YOUR CHEST!

AND NOW TO TRY OUT MY NEW STRENGTH!

NNNNNG!

HMM — SET MY SIGHTS TOO HIGH!

I'LL TRY THIS ONE!

NNNNNG!

SOMETHING SMALLER...

PERHAPS THIS ONE?

THUD!

I'VE DONE IT! I'M A SUPERMAN!!!

AMAZING!

40

I GIVE IN! GIVE ME THE ANTIDOTE AND YOU CAN GO FREE!

TRY A HAIR OF THE DOG?

GETAFIX MAY NOT REMEMBER THE ANTIDOTE...

HE'S A BIT HARE-BRAINED SOMETIMES!

HO! HO! HO!

DON'T DISTRESS YOURSELF! WE AGREE!

I'LL HAVE TO GO AND FETCH INGREDIENTS FROM THE FOREST...

I'LL ARRANGE FOR AN ESCORT...

!

I MAY NOT HAVE THE SECRET OF THE MAGIC POTION, BUT AS SOON AS I'VE GOT RID OF THIS HAIR I'LL WIPE OUT THOSE TWO GAULS. IT WILL GIVE ME MORAL SATISFACTION!

WHY WERE YOU SO QUICK TO ACCEPT HIS OFFER? THAT CENTURION MEANS MISCHIEF!

THE EFFECTS OF THE HAIR LOTION DON'T LAST LONG ...

TOMORROW THEIR HAIR WILL HAVE STOPPED GROWING. I MUST THINK OF A WAY OUT OF THIS!

REPORTING TO ESCORT YOU TO THE FOREST FOR INGREDIENTS!

STOP WALKING ON MY HAIR!

WELL, PICK IT UP, THEN!

I HAVE A PLAN!

THAT'S OUR STRONG POINT, WE'RE BURSTING WITH IDEAS!

42

44

LET GO!

RIGHT!

BOING!

COME ON! LET'S GO BEFORE THEY COME ROUND!

JUST AS I WAS BEGINNING TO ENJOY MYSELF!

VADE RETRO!!

TCHOP!

ROMANS!

HEAPS OF ROMANS!

THERE ARE MORE OVER THERE TOO!

AND OVER THERE! WE'RE SURROUNDED!

REINFORCEMENTS ARRIVING IN THE NICK OF TIME!

WE'RE IN A SPOT!

CRISMUS BONUS WAS EXTREMELY EAGER TO GET HOLD OF THE RECIPE FOR A MAGIC POTION WHICH WOULD HAVE MADE HIM INVINCIBLE, REMOVING ALL OBSTACLES BETWEEN HIMSELF AND THE IMPERIAL THRONE...

AND ALL NIGHT LONG BY THE LIGHT OF THE MOON, UNDER A STARRY SKY, THE GAULS FEAST THEIR HEROES, VICTORIOUS OVER THEIR ENEMIES THANKS TO MAGIC, THE PROTECTION OF THE GODS, AND LOW CUNNING...

PRINTED IN BELGIUM BY
proost
INTERNATIONAL BOOK PRODUCTION

PRINTED IN BELGIUM